50 Easy Exercises to Get Your Toddler Talking

Designed by a Speech-Language Pathologist

Freya Magennis

D1565315

Find Freya at:
https://www.happierwithtea.com/

Contents

INTRODUCTION

Welcome to '50 Easy Exercises to Get Your Toddler Talking.' As a registered and experienced Speech and Language Pathologist, this is an area that I am passionate about! I believe firmly in creating a great space for conversations, and making interactions fun so your toddler is motivated to join in.

These fifty exercises are designed with one aim: to get your toddler talking! Whether you want to help them to say their first words or to give their language a boost, these exercises are just what you need. The exercises are grouped in the following sections:

EXERCISES TO BUILD LISTENING SKILLS
EXERCISES FOR FIRST WORDS
EXERCISES TO BUILD VOCABULARY
EXERCISES TO BUILD UNDERSTANDING
EXERCISES WITH FLASHCARDS
EXERCISES TO BUILD GRAMMAR
EXERCISES TO BUILD LANGUAGE IN EVERYDAY LIFE
EXERCISES FOR EARLY READING SKILLS

Exercises are a fantastic way to teach language and to get your toddler talking! When you do exercises that are fun and motivating for your child, you create a rich language environment where your child is interested and engaged. The exercises provide a focus for you to teach your child new skills, and gives them a space to practice.

Repetition is important in learning these new skills, so don't worry about doing your child's favorite exercises over and over if that's what they want. Feel free to pick and choose the ones that work best for you, your child and your family.

These exercises are designed so that you can easily adjust the level to the level of your child. Where appropriate, I have suggested ways that you can do the exercise at a lower or higher level of language so it's just right for your child, no matter how much talking they're already doing.

If your toddler is not yet talking, these exercises combined with the language strategies will boost their language. Hopefully it won't be long until they're saying those first words! If your toddler is already talking, these exercises will grow and develop their language skills.

Above all, these exercises are designed to be fun! That's how children learn best!

Enjoy!

Freya

KEY STRATEGIES

Remember that YOU are the biggest factor in your child's language development. You can have a huge impact on your child's ability to understand and use language. The following strategies will make a big difference and can be used as part of everyday life in all of your interactions with your child.

Let your child lead the interaction. Watch and see what they are interested in. They might start an interaction by pointing at something, by making a sound, or saying a word. Your child is showing what they are engaged with. Feed in language related to this thing. They are much more likely to listen and absorb new words when they are engaged and interested in the topic. This is true for every situation- when you are out on a walk, playing with toys, or open a picture book. Hold back for a moment and let your child lead the way.

Use your child's name to get their attention before you speak. Ask them to stop what they are doing to listen to an instruction, it is difficult to 'listen and do' at the same time.

Comment don't question when talking to your child. Instead of asking questions or asking them to name things, constantly give them the words for things. This will reduce pressure and will build their understanding. It's like a sponge- instead of trying to squeeze language out from them, focus on feeding it in.

Give your child time when you're talking. After you make a comment to them, or ask a question, wait for about five seconds before saying something else. This space in the conversation takes away pressure and gives them time to process your language. It will be much more likely that they will say something back.

Expand the words your child uses. For example, if they make a sound, say the word for them. If they say one word (e.g. 'dog'), expand this and say back two words for them (e.g. 'a big dog,' or, 'the dog is running.') Make sure your sentences are grammatical and you include all the little in between words. When your child puts two words together (e.g. big dog') you might expand this into three- ('the big dog is hairy!') When you do this, you are showing your child the next step in language development, and helping them to reach it.

Repeat back the correct form when your child makes mistakes. This will show your child that you are listening and interested. It gives you the chance to repeat back what they have said in the correct form. For example, if they say, 'mouses!' you can say, 'yeah, mice! Lots of mice. Mice.' You are modelling the correct form in a natural way that will allow the interaction to continue.

EXERCISES TO BUILD LISTENING SKILLS

These exercises are designed to build listening skills. Attention and listening is a foundational skill for language. We watch babies develop this as they start to focus on their parents' faces, respond to sounds, and start to respond to their own name. In a few years they will be able to listen attentively to stories, listen to their friends, and because they are able to listen, they will know how to respond. Language isn't possible without a strong foundation of attention and listening.

Find the Sound

Find the Sound is a fun way to build listening skills. Get a toy or piece of equipment that makes a noise. Wind up or musical toys can work well for this, or even general household items such as an egg timer or metronome. Ask your child to close their eyes, and hide the item somewhere in the room- e.g. under a cushion, behind the door. This helps children to learn to listen. To make it more challenging, try turning the sound down so it's even quieter. This is a game for younger children and is great for building attention and listening which are foundational skills for language. You can even use this with babies- put the object somewhere around the room and see if they turn their head to find the sound. If they don't, you can make it obvious and point at it saying, "Wow! Can you hear the music? It's there!"

Listening Walk

Going on a Listening Walk is a fun way to cue your child into listening carefully for things around them. Tell them that you are going to go on a walk, and you are both going to listen carefully for sounds that you hear.

This might be things such as the wind, birds, crickets, neighbors, cars, animals, or anything else in your vicinity.

Initially, you might need to point out some sounds to your child as they may not be cued into quieter sounds. When they do point something out, give them lots of specific praise for 'great listening!'

Stop and Go

Stop and Go is a fun active game for kids. The basic principle is that when you say 'go', they can run around. They have to listen out for the word 'stop' which means they have to stop and freeze in place immediately.

To make this game even more beneficial, why not give them different variations when you say 'go.' You might say, 'ok this time when I say 'go' I want you to walk like you're tigers/ ballerinas/ hop on one foot/ walk backwards,' or anything else you can think of.

When you say 'stop' you could walk around to check that they are being perfectly still. If you are playing with a group of kids, you could eliminate anyone who moves or wobbles.

Old McDonald Listening Game

Get pictures of different animals and lay them out. Tell your child to listen very carefully for each animal and to hold it up when they hear it. Sing Old McDonald and as you go through the animals, help your child to listen out and hold up the picture of each animal as they hear it.

At the start, you might need to make this very obvious by emphasizing the animal and looking at your child meaningfully. However, as they get better, you can start to make it more challenging to build their listening skills- you could even whisper the name of the animal so they have to listen very carefully.

This game works incredibly well with a small group of children, as you can put one animal in front of each and tell them to just listen out for their animal and hold it up when they hear it.

Remember to give specific praise for 'great listening.'

EXERCISES TO ENCOURAGE FIRST WORDS

Your child's first word is a moment all parents are super excited about! As understanding of language grows, your child's use of language will start to develop. At the beginning, your child expresses themselves with sounds and babbling, but before long they are using single words and then full sentences. When you are encouraging first words, pick ones that are motivating. Also pick words where there is the opportunity to use it in lots of ways throughout the day. Aim to repeat it lots and lots in different contexts all through the day.

Catch the Gap

Catch the Gap is a clever game to help your child to say their very first words. Understanding comes before talking, so teach your child lots of nursery rhymes. Don't be afraid to be very repetitive.

The Catch the Gap exercise is when you say the Nursery Rhyme that your toddler is now familiar with, but then stop just before saying the last word in a line.

Look at your toddler and show on your face that you're encouraging them to finish the line.

For example, you could say:

Incy Wincy Spider climbed up the waterspout

Down came the rain and washed the spider.... (out)

If your child doesn't say the last word, pause for just a few seconds, and then say it for them and continue with the rhyme. Don't be put off- persist with this strategy.

Rhymes are engaging and fun and toddlers become very familiar with them easily so it's a lovely easy way for them to say their first words.

Phrase Completion

Phrase Completion is another easy, low-pressure way to help your child say their first words.

It's a little like Catch the Gap but without the rhymes.

Simply say a phrase (pick one that your child is familiar with) and stop before saying the last word.

For example, you might say:

Go to (bed)

Let's brush your (teeth/ hair)

Open the (door)

Use phrases that you find yourself saying everyday to your toddler. Do phrase completion in context (e.g. while holding the item) and make it very obvious with your voice. Make your voice rise at the end so it's clear that another word is coming and give lots of eye contact and smile to show your toddler you want them to finish your sentence.

EXERCISES TO BUILD VOCABULARY

A strong vocabulary is needed for great conversations, to engage with friends, and for learning across all subjects in school. Remember that vocabulary is not just made up from naming words. To expand your child's vocabulary, choose lots of different types of words- action words, describing words, location words and emotion words. Your child will need all of them to be able to engage in conversations. Books are a great way to teach vocabulary that might not come up in everyday life (such as jungle animals). These exercises will help you to teach your child new and interesting words.

Sort by Color

Sort by Color is a sorting exercise that is suitable for any child just learning their colors. Decide on two colors that you want to teach. Choose a variety of objects that are on or other of these colors, and then help your child to sort them into two piles.

Ensure that when you do this, you keep repeating the color over and over, e.g. 'yes that's right, that one's red.' Resist the temptation to ask, 'what color is that?' Remember that you want to feed in the language instead of squeezing it out.

Start with two colors and then gradually build up to three and even four or five.

A variation of this game could be to go on a 'Color Hunt' around the house. Choose a color and then find objects that are this color. You can model the language 'light' and 'dark' for your child once they're becoming confident with color names. You could say, 'yes that's green. It's a dark green.'

Sort by Texture

You can teach children about textures with a sorting exercise. Collect objects that are either rough or smooth and then help your child to sort into two piles. You can talk about materials here too. For example, 'yes this is smooth. This one is made of metal' or 'this wood is rough.' Other textures can include, "hard", "soft", "liquid", "solid", "lumpy", and "gritty." Repeat the texture that you are teaching a few times to help your child remember it. If possible, use the texture from the game in everyday life- point out things with different textures and get your child to feel it. Remember to keep feeding language in instead of squeezing the language out through asking questions.

What's My Man Missing? (Body Parts)

This is a lovely game that's fantastic for teaching body parts. Draw two men side by side. On one drawing, leave out a body part such as an arm or the head. Ask your child, 'what's my man missing?'

They might know the word, or if they don't they can point at the first man to show. When they do this, feed in the language of the body part. Repeat it two or three times so they really hear it and will start to remember it.

Don't be afraid to make your missing body parts more and more obscure once your child is confident with basic body parts. You could leave out the elbow, the knee, an eyebrow- get creative! Initially, your child will give the general area such as 'leg.' You can say, 'that's right. He's missing part of his leg. That part is called the knee. He's missing his knee! Can you show me your knee?'

Feely Bag

The Feely Bag Game can be used to teach a range of new words. Start by putting just one 'secret object' into a bag. Let your child put their hand in and feel the object. Ask them to describe the object they feel. If they are having difficulty with this, you can give them choices, 'is it rough or smooth? / is it big or small? / is it round or square? / is it hard or soft?' Choices are a brilliant way to help your child to express themselves if they are having trouble. It is much less pressure than a direct question ('how does it feel?') if they have limited language. Once your child has described it, see if they can guess what it is. Pull it out and see if they were right!

You can also reverse this game by asking your child to put something in the bag (this could be from a choice of 10 things that you have selected) and then you can describe the object and guess what it is. Your child will love watching you try to guess, and it's a brilliant opportunity to feed in language ('wow, it's really big, and it feels spiky! I wonder what it is...')

Emotions Game

The emotions game is a simple way to introduce and start to teach the words for various emotions. Simply make a face and ask your child to label the motion.

It might sound a little complicated, but start with the most basic emotions- happy and sad. Add in angry and scared when you're ready. And then you can move onto other ones such as bored, worried, nervous, excited etc. When you are first teaching these to your child, try giving a choice. For example you might say, 'OK ready- look at my face- am I happy or sad?' The choice makes it a lot easier than simply asking your child to name the emotion.

Encourage them to make a face and you will guess which emotion they are trying to show.

This is a game for you to clown around with! Don't take it too seriously.

It's great for starting to teach emotional vocabulary which is a key component in developing emotional literacy. To take it further, name emotions that your toddler is showing in everyday life (e.g. 'aw you look sad about that'). Also label emotions that you see in other people and in characters on tv and in books. Also say why they're feeling like that and what they can do. Emotional literacy is one of the most important life skills that your child will develop!

I Spy

I Spy is a classic game that is actually a great tool for teaching new vocabulary. For a younger child, don't use the first letter as this is likely to be far too hard. Instead, you could use I Spy to describe the object or even describe the function.

For example, I spy with my little eye-

Something that is really hot

Something that is blue

Something that says 'meow'

Something that is used for eating

Something that is really big

This is a great game for the car or when you are out and about for a walk.

Where is it?

'Where is it?' is a fun way to teach location words (prepositions). The most common location words are:
In, on, below, under, beside, in front of, behind, and inside.
Simply take turns putting a toy beside/ inside etc. a box or a basket. Ask your child, 'where is it?' and help them to answer- e.g. it's inside the box. Take turns placing the object and describing where it is.
Start with teaching just two of these words- in front and behind are nice ones to start with, and add more as your child becomes confident with these.
You can use objects based around their interests- e.g. beside the truck/ behind the truck.
These words are important to learn for subjects such as early mathematics in school.

Shopping Game

This shopping game will build your child's vocabulary and also help them to understand categories.
Get lots of pictures of shopping items. The best way to do this is to get a shopping leaflet from a supermarket and cut out lots of the pictures.
Tell your child you're going to 'put away the shopping.'
You could draw out a fridge, a cupboard, a freezer and a fruit bowl- whatever is appropriate for your house.

Then sort out the shopping together. Describe the items as you go. For example, 'oh look- ice cream! That's really cold! Where should we put it?'

Be careful not to turn this game into a test for your child, but to model as much language as you can.

Feed in, don't squeeze out!

Shopping Cart Bingo

Shopping Cart Bingo is a second game that you can play with your shopping magazine pictures- this time you will need two pictures of each item.

Give your child 4 random items for their 'shopping list'. Take four different items for yourself.

Then spread out a selection of items (including the 8 from the shopping lists) face down on the table.

Take turns to pick an item. If it matches with an item on your shopping list, then you can keep it. If it doesn't, you have to put it back and it is the other person's turn.

The first person to get all the items from their shopping list is the winner.

Set the rule that when you pick a card up, you must say the name of the item. It's ok if your child doesn't know the name; you can say the word for them. The more times they hear it, the more likely they are to understand the meaning and soon to say it for themselves!

Picture Jigsaw

Find a simple picture from a magazine (or print one off), and cut it into four pieces. Your child can piece it together and then name what is on the picture.

This will work best if you choose pictures of things they are starting to know the name for, or a target word that you would like to teach them.

As your child gets better at this, you can make the puzzle more pieces.

Remember to model the word for them as well instead of asking, 'what's that?' This will build their understanding and vocabulary.

This game will also build their cognitive skills.

Photo Diary

Making a photo book works especially well to teach location words such as: under, beside, in, on, behind.

You can also use it to teach action words such as: jump, skip, run, hop, stand, stretch, roll.

Have fun with your child when you're making the photobook- get them to go 'under' the chair- show them what this means. Then, take a picture to demonstrate each word.

You can print the pictures off with the words underneath.

For example: Molly is under the chair/ Molly is behind the chair/ Molly is stretching.

Staple or ring-bind them together so they are in one book. Then read through the book with your child, reading out the words and emphasizing the new words. The book will likely be very motivating for your child as it contains pictures of them. They are likely to go back to the book again and again. Remember that as you look at the pictures together, keep feeding the words in.

You can use this idea to teach lots of other new words, too. This is a great way to teach colors.

Have a Theme Day

A theme day is a really cool way to develop language in everyday life. This can be used to teach or further consolidate words that you have been teaching or focusing on. It is also brilliant for when your child has a special interest in something, as they will be very engaged and motivated to learn new words in this area.

Pick the theme that your child is engaged in and brainstorm lots of words and conversations you could have around this theme. Also pick some activities that would tie in well- most of the ideas in this book could be used around a particular theme.

It could include: crafts, outfits, baking, games, and even role play or puppets. Teach the target words in natural ways through conversations that are around the theme.

Above all, have fun! This is when your child will learn best.

Set Up Role Plays

Since your kids aren't getting out and about in the world, set up role plays at home.

Kids love trying out 'adult' world things such as playing shop, school, doctors, or vets. It's actually a time where they learn a lot!

Don't be scared of getting involved and playing alongside, or even suggesting the game in the first place! You might need to help your kids to plan the steps on how to do it. Help them to assign roles, and also gently teach social skills if you have more than one child (e.g. taking turns and sharing). You could also playfully introduce a problem ('oh no! We're out of eggs! What should we do?") This will develop your child's problem-solving skills.

EXERCISES TO BUILD UNDERSTANDING

With a strong foundation of attention and play, your child will be developing their understanding of language. Children need to be able to understand words well before they will start to use them for themselves. It's like learning a foreign language as an adult- you can't open your mouth and communicate until you understand the words you can use. Generally, children also understand more language than they can say, and the more they understand, the more they will soon say! These exercises are designed to build your child's understanding of language.

Barrier Game

A Barrier Game is a fun way to give your child practice in both giving and receiving instructions. The basic idea is to have matching pictures or objects in front of each of you with a barrier in between so you can't see each other's things. It might be that you each have an uncolored picture of a house in front of you, or you could each have a few toys: a teddy, a spoon and a bed. The barrier might be a hardback book standing up, or even a piece of cardboard.

Take turns to give each other instructions. For example, you might say, 'color the door of the house red.' Or, if you have toys you could say, 'put teddy under the bed.'

Then, when you are ready, take away the barrier and see if your pictures or toys match.

Depending on your child's age and stage of development, you might need to make your instructions very simple, and check after each one. You might even need to give cues (such as showing 'under' with your hand). As you practice, you can start to reduce these.

If your child is older, try giving a series of instructions before checking to see if it matches. Also give them a chance to give you the instructions to follow.

Obstacle Course

Set up an obstacle course in the house or garden and tell your child to listen carefully for the instructions.

Give a few instructions for your child to follow out.

For example, this might be, 'crawl under the chair, run around it twice, run backwards to the tennis ball, and then roll it into the bucket.'

You can adjust this game so it's fun for any age. For a younger child, give simple instructions and give one at a time.

For an older child, you can give longer instructions, and you can also make it fun by timing it and seeing if they can beat their time. Or, you could have a target at the end- throwing a ball into a bucket or kicking it into a goal. Making this a little more challenging can make it much more exciting for your child.

Object Hunt

An indoor hunt for kids doesn't have to be a full-scale Scavenger Hunt which takes a big amount of preparation. A simpler idea is to make a list for your kids of things to find and then let them head off to hunt the objects. These could be texture related (something smooth/rough), color (something that's dark blue/ something that has two colors on it), sound related (something that's begins with the 'sss' sound) and even function related (something that you use to stick things). It can be anything that you choose. You could reward your child for finding everything on the list.

EXERCISES WITH FLASHCARDS

Flashcards are fantastic. They allow you to choose the words you want to teach, and to play lots of different and fun games. They are great for teaching games with turn-taking and simple 'rules', such as 'Go Fish' or 'Snap.'

Flashcards are just one piece of the puzzle in learning new words. Children learn best through real life experiences. It might be helpful to jot down the words used in your flashcards, and then use them in a variety of contexts throughout the week. Repeat the words in new contexts- this will broaden their understanding of a word. When children understand a word really well, then they will start to use it!

When you are choosing words for your flashcards, choose a variety of words. Try to choose words that are interesting and meaningful for your child.

Torch Card Hunt

This game works well for teaching animals and can be set up to a 'night safari.' Print a few cards with animals (or cut out from magazines). Stick them around the room. Close all the curtains and turn out the lights, then give your child a torch and tell them you're going on a safari adventure.

Shine the light around and when the beam lands on an animal, name it. Again, let your child name it if they know, and label it for them if they can't. You can add an extra word or two to what they say. For example, if they say 'tiger' you can say, 'yes it's a scary tiger!' Go along with your child and help to make it exciting and fun. This will help your child to be interested and engaged, and will help them to remember the words.

Bean Bag Toss

Pick a few flashcards with vocabulary that you want to teach your child. Space the cards out on the ground at various distances. This works fine as an inside game but it is also a great game to do outdoors! When you are first teaching new words, make it easy, and keep it to a choice of two cards. Give your child a beanbag, and then tell them to listen carefully and throw to the word they hear. Reinforce by naming the word a few times. 'Yeah- you heard 'elephant' and you threw to the elephant- good listening!' Increase the number of cards to three or even four.

You can also make this fun by putting hula hoops around the cards- your child has to get the beanbag inside the hoop. When it gets too easy, make it harder by moving the cards further away.

You can also let your child have a turn at telling you which one to throw towards. Help them as much as they need. You might need to say, 'do you want me to throw towards the turtle or the fish?' This way, you're giving them the answer and giving them the words when they don't know it for themselves. When you throw it, ask, 'was I right? Did I throw it at the elephant?' By doing this your child is hearing the word over and over again and becoming more and familiar with it.

Card Hop

Card Hop is another fun way to make flashcards interesting and teach vocabulary. If you want to get fancy, you can draw out lily pads to put the cards on. Otherwise, just lay them out on the ground. Tell your child you are going to hop and name the cards as you land on them. This is a fun way to learn vocabulary as you are making it physical and using more parts of the brain. Your child will be interested, engaged, and having fun. All of this can help them to learn and remember the words.

Different variations of this game include moving to the cards in different ways- jump, hop, skip or even go backwards. Pretending the floor is lava or crocodile infested water will build your child's imagination at the same time.

Bottle Cap Game

The Bottle Cap Game is another variation on the flashcard games. To play this game, have about three flashcards picked out with words that you want to teach. Remember that it doesn't have to be just naming words but it can be any words- action words, or description words work well. Have three bottle caps and stick the cards to the tops (smaller works better). Alternatively, you could stick the cards to jam jar lids. Find something to hide under the bottle caps or lids- this might be a coin or even paperclip (be careful with small objects if you have a younger child as they are a choking risk!)

Ask your child to close their eyes, put the object under one of the caps, and then let them guess where it is. Teach them to say the word on the flashcard before lifting up to check. For example, if you are teaching action words and have flashcards of sitting, eating and running, they might say 'eating' and then look under to see if they're right, or they might say, 'is it under eating?' if their language is at a higher level.

Your child will need help to do this as they will just be excited to guess and won't name the card unless you teach them the 'rules.' They can then have a turn at hiding the object and you can model, 'hmm is it under eating?'

Building Game

Another variation of using flashcards to teach language, the building game is great for kids who love blocks, bricks, Lego and stacking. Stick a flashcard onto each block, and then prompt your child to name it before they stack it.

You could take turns to stack the cards. This will let you to model the vocabulary you are teaching through the flashcards. See how high you can make the tower.

You can also model words such as 'taller,' 'bigger,' 'wobbly' and 'your turn', 'my turn.'

And, of course, the best part about building a tower is knocking it down when you have finished!

Fishing Game

To play the fishing game, simply attach a paper clip to each flashcard you are using. If you want to be fancy, you can make fish pictures to stick to the backs of the cards. Then make your 'fishing rod'- use any length of material and tie a string to it that has a magnet on the end. Strew the cards around on the floor and then go fishing to catch the cards with your rod. Remember that when they 'catch a fish' they need to name the picture on the card. This is a fantastic game that kids absolutely love. You can turn it into a turn-taking game and teach your child these early social skills. Model the words: 'my turn' and 'your turn.'

Hide and Seek with Cards

This is a super simple and fun way to play with flashcards. All you need to do is choose the vocabulary that you want to teach (remember that it doesn't have to be fancy designed flash cards, but cut out pictures from magazines, printed and cut pictures, or even your own drawn pictures can work, too), and then hide them around the room for your child to find.

Make sure that when they find it, name it for them! Don't worry about asking, 'what's that?' If they know, they will say. Focus on feeding in language and saying the word lots of times. Also swap roles and give them a chance to hide the cards for you.

Depending on the age of your child, this can provide hours of fun.

Bag of Cards

Bag of Cards is just about as simple as it sounds. Get a bright, colorful interesting bag for your cards, or even make your own. The action of reaching in and drawing out a mystery card is actually very fun for kids. Make sure they name what they get!

To make this a little more interesting, you could transform it into a 'bingo' game. Have a board (two by two, three by three or whatever size works for you) with four random copies of the cards inside the bag- you and your child will have different ones. Take turns to draw a card out, name it, and then see if it matches with the cards in front of you. The first one to fill their board/ get a straight line is the winner!

Go Fish

Go Fish is a classic but easy card game that can easily be played with flashcards. You will need to prepare a set that has two of each picture. You can play with almost any amount of cards, just modify the rules to suit what you have. Deal out five cards each to start with. Help your child to match any pairs they may have. Then, take turns asking each other, 'do you have apple?' (if you are teaching food or fruit vocabulary). If the person has it they need to hand it over. If they don't they say, 'Go Fish,' and the person who asked the question picks a card up from the pile. At the end, the person with the most pairs wins.

You can easily include other siblings in this game. I like it because the phrase 'Go Fish' is used over and over- repetition is great for learning language. Also remember to name what's on the card as much as you can.

If your child is a little younger, they can play this game but another parent or older sibling might need to play along with them.

Memory

I have found memory to be the most popular game that I have introduced in therapy! Again, you will need two pictures of each card. Simply put them face down on the table, and then take turns to turn over two cards on the table. The goal is to start to remember where the cards are. At the end, the person with the most pairs is the winner.

When you play this game, you will most likely need to slow your child down! This is just because the visual matching is so exciting! They are likely to turn the cards over quickly without naming them, and then rely on their visual skills to match them. While this game is good for building these skills, introduce it as a rule from the very beginning that for every card you turn over, you name what's on it. Do this for your turn as well. Go slow and as you turn over each card say, 'oh, it's a bear!' or whatever is on the card! You may need to prompt your child to actually name the cards.

Post It

Posting is incredibly motivating for kids. Used by itself, you would simply ask your child to name the card and then post it. For a post-box, consider using an old box with a slot cut out- this might be a cereal box or a tub. You can decorate the box to make it fun, and even consider drawing a face on the cereal box so that your toddler posts into an animal's or a person's mouth.

To make this more interesting, you can add physical activity in. For example, you could set up a little obstacle course for your child with the post box at the end. Or they could earn the cards. For example, if they knock over a plastic bottle with a beanbag, they get a card to post.

Remember to prompt them to name what's on the card before posting it in.

EXERCISES TO BUILD GRAMMAR

Grammar is the way in which we use words to say exactly what we mean. If we don't use the correct word ending, tenses, and pronouns, we will change the meaning of what we say. For example, 'I walked' vs 'I am walking'. Grammar is crucial for kids to develop and use correctly. However, it is a little like icing on the cake.

There are so many skills that need to be in place before grammar can develop. These include: attention and listening, play skills, understanding and use of language. The stronger these foundational skills are for your child, the more opportunities they will have to fine tune their grammar.

However, if these foundational skills are already strong and you want to give your child's grammar development an extra boost, you can do some focused practice with exercises like these. These exercises are for the earliest stages of grammar-pronouns, plurals, and basic past tense.

He is/She is

Pronouns can be quite tricky for kids to develop. Initially, they might say, 'boy walk' instead of 'the boy is walking.' While a top tip is to model back the correct version naturally without correcting your child, this pronoun game is also a good way to give your child some extra practice.

Look through a sport, gardening or children's magazine and cut out lots of pictures of males and females. Then sort them into two piles, the 'he is...' pile and the 'she is' pile. Teach your child to say, 'he is swimming', or 'she is walking.' Take a turn in the game yourself and model this grammar- let your child hear it lots of times. Then also use it in real life whenever you get the chance- point out and comment about 'he' and 'she', emphasizing the words a little.

This also helps your child to practice the −ing verb endings.

This exercise alongside practice in everyday life will help your child to develop these grammatical structures in no time!

Before and After Cards

Use the internet to find before and after pictures or take your own photos! Make sure the photos demonstrate both the before and after with the grammar for each. You can make these into a photo-book with the target grammar in the words underneath.

Start with regular grammar rules before moving to irregular.

The before and after cards could include:

Past Tense- (Teach the −ed ending first). Example: I am jumping- I jumped/ I am walking- I walked.

Plurals- (Teach the −s ending first). Example: one cow- two cows/ one horse- two horses.

Some irregular grammatical structures could include:

I am eating- I ate

I am drawing- I drew

I am driving- I drove
One mouse- two mice
One tooth- two teeth
One person- two people

EXERCISES TO BUILD LANGUAGE IN EVERYDAY LIFE

Children learn language from listening to language. Children absorb the language spoken by their parents, siblings and the other people around them.

You are the most important person in your child's life as they learn to speak and to understand what is said to them.

Children need to hear language over and over again for months and years before they will start to use it for themselves. I believe that it is crucially important for parents to understand their irreplaceable role in the language development of their child. You are the single most important person in their language development. The strategies you use in everyday life to build your child's language will have the biggest impact on their speech and language development.

Use these exercises to build language in everyday interactions.

Feed in Words in Everyday Routines

The goal is to feed language in, don't squeeze it out. Aim to teach, not test.

Look for opportunities in everyday life to feed language in. You can do this by naming things around you.

Be careful not to keep asking your child questions as this can make a conversation more pressure than it needs to be. Feeding language in is much less pressure and will help your child to hear the words more often- they will be much more likely to truly learn the words.

Start to notice the ratio of questions to comments that you use, and the effect that this has.

You can easily flip your question into a comment. Instead of asking, "what are you doing?" you might say, "Wow, you're jumping in puddles!" If you're reading a book, instead of asking "what's the bear doing?" you could say, "Look, the bear is eating a fish."

See if you can make four comments before asking a question. And remember to give lots of wait time after each comment- count to at least five in your head. This gives your child a chance to join in the conversation if they want to. Often it's when the pressure is off that kids will become really chatty and use lots of language.

Go on a Nature Walk

There are different ways to do a nature walk and make it fun. You could send your child around the garden with a list of things to collect (e.g. a leaf, a twig etc.), a list of things to take photos of (a bug, a bird, a tree, a flower), or even just give them a list of items that they can tick off as they see. You could let them stick some of the things they collected into a scrap book. They could even draw something that they saw (e.g. a bug, a flower or a spider's web).

Become a Commentator

Labelling what is happening, what your child is doing, what you are doing, and what you see is a great way to tick these boxes.

We can get used to moving about tasks quickly and efficiently, juggling the kids, the dishes, and the laundry.

One of the easiest things you can add into your busy routine is to have a commentator mentality by adding language into your everyday experiences. As your child reaches for a spoon, you might say, 'You want a spoon. Spoon.' As you are washing your child, you might say, 'I'm washing your arm. Now I'm washing your other arm!'

It's important to model a whole variety of words. Don't just name things, but describe them- use actions (jumping, eating, flying), locations (beside, behind, in front of), pronouns (he, she, they).

Your child won't learn this word from hearing it once. As you repeat it (say it at least 2 or 3 times each time) in a variety of contexts and environments, your child will slowly build a good understanding of the word and all its nuances. Soon they will start to use it in their own language.

Give Choices

Giving choices is another fantastic opportunity for you to feed in words to develop your child's speech and language.

If you ask your child, "do you want a banana?" you are likely to get a mono-syllabic "yes" or "no" as a response. On the other hand, if you ask, "what do you want?" your child might not yet know the words to use to answer. If this is the case, giving a choice is a perfect balance.

If you ask your child, "would you like a banana or an apple?" you have provided the vocabulary that they need to answer the question.

You are helping them to experience success and you have also fed language in- each time you do this, your child will become more and more familiar with the vocabulary needed in different contexts.

Again, you can use this at different levels. It might be that your child can name lots of objects, but can't yet describe them. In this case, if offering a toy or food, you could say, "do you want the big one or the small one?"

You have provided your child with the vocabulary that they need to answer your question successfully, and you are extending their language beyond a yes or no answer.

Use Communication Temptations

Give your child communication temptations to give them a reason to communicate. It's important that you do this both gently and playfully, without getting to the point where your child is frustrated or upset.

So how does it work? One example is snack time. You could give your child the cup but 'forget' to put the juice in it. When he protests, you can continue to act stupid and say, 'what is it? What do you want?'

Your child might say the word at this point, or they might hold out the object to you, or just make a noise. It is important to take any communication as an attempt. Your expectations need to be realistic, but you are helping them to reach a level that you already know they can achieve.

Give your child a packet without automatically opening it for them. Wait for them to come to you to request this. Again, they might request with a gesture, a noise, or using words. You can model, "oh open."

Set out a race track but 'forget' to immediately provide the cars.

When helping your child get ready in the morning, you might put one sock and shoe on and say, "OK, we're ready- let's go!"

When they empty a bowl or cup, do not instantly refill but wait for them to communicate. You can model the word, "more."

Use Puppets and Dolls

Use puppets and dolls to act out stories and conversations. This will give a massive boost to your child's language. You can act out scenes from books you're reading, stories you've told, or even everyday interactions.

An example of this is to use puppets and dolls to act out going to the doctor. Model the language used in this situation ('Uhoh teddy is sick, what should we do?')

Prompt your child to problem-solve and imagine.

Through doing this, you will develop your child's play skills, social skills, cognitive and language levels.

Play is the place that children explore and learn about the world. Using puppets and dolls gives you a chance to feed in language, and allows them to explore and learn about new things.

Shared Book Reading

If the foundation of teaching your toddler to read involves building their language, then it can be helpful to think of it as a conversation.

To make the most of the opportunities to build language, allow the conversation to develop naturally. It's ok to go off topic from the book and the words that are written.

Use it as an opportunity to extend the topic. You can do this by giving more information- match this to the level your child is at. You can also extend the topic by prompting your child to think beyond the here and now.

A question such as, "what do you think will happen next" can develop problem-solving and predicting skills.

A comment such as, "the boy looks really sad. I wonder what he's thinking," can develop skills such as theory of mind– understanding another person's perspective and starting to build your toddler's emotional literacy. Talk about feelings, emotions and opinions.

This is an invaluable teaching time that will massively help your toddler to learn to read. It will help them make the jump to literacy and they will have a huge advantage as they will have a much better understanding of what they are reading.

Pretend Play

When your child is little, it is important to join in playfully with your child. Show your child how to play with objects, and what actions they can use. You can start to use simple pretend language, "let's pretend we're on a train."

You can gradually start to introduce symbolic objects– or even pretend you have an object when you really don't have anything. Teach your child explicitly how to do this, "are you a doctor? Let's pretend you have a stethoscope."

Later, you can support your child to act out a story, but don't be afraid to throw in a problem that you'll have to solve together, "oh no! How will swim to the island with all of these sharks in the water?!"

When you have got your child and peers started in this kind of play, don't be afraid to step out and allow them to take the game in new directions.

Your role is to suggest new ideas or to coach your child to extend their thinking and level of play, but it still needs to be playful and fun- no pressure!

Expand their Words

Expanding is all about your language being one step above the language that your child is using.

When your child starts to use single words, and they point at the cat and say, "cat", you might reply, "Ooh a big cat" or you could say, "The cat is sleeping." Slightly emphasize the new word, and repeat your statement two or three times. This is also a good time to teach your child different types of words- describing words, action words, pronouns.

Also remember that the little grammatical words are still important for your child to hear, even if they are not using them yet. It's better for them to hear "the cat is sleeping" than "cat sleeping" as the second example is grammatically incorrect.

Even when your child is using full sentences, you can continue to expand their language. For example, if they say, "look! A big scary spider!" You could reply, "yes, the big scary spider is scuttling on the ceiling" or you could add a new idea such as, "yes, it's a big scary spider. I wonder if he is scared of us."

Model don't Correct

Modelling is one of the key strategies to boost your child's speech and language when you notice that they are making mistakes or when these mistakes become obvious.

If your child says, "look, two horse!"

You can respond, "yes, two horses! There are two horses. Horses."

By responding in this way, you have:

Listened to your child and affirmed what they wanted to say.

You have repeated the correct word a few times for them to hear.

Allowed them to hear the correct version in a very relaxed way- you have repeated it and reinforced it.

You have not put any pressure on them or on the conversation.

This is crucially important. Correcting your child draws their attention to errors; you are reinforcing their initial error by letting them hear it again.

Children learn when communication is positive and natural. Ideally, your child won't even notice that they are being corrected!

EXERCISES FOR EARLY READING SKILLS

As parents, we want to know how to teach our toddler to read. We want them to start off school on a strong foundation to have every advantage for academic success. Literacy is more and more important in the modern world. Even in a job that doesn't revolve around it, we still need to be able to fill in forms, read instructions, and generally have enough literacy to get online or to deal with banks and other organizations.

These exercises will help you to develop early reading skills for your child.

Rhymes

Back to basics: teach your child Nursery Rhymes and read simple rhyming books with them.

Repetition is key- nursery rhymes are entertaining, predictable, and very easy to repeat over and over. They are especially useful for teaching the foundations of phonological awareness, especially rhyme.

Your natural voice is always much better than a recording- you can speed up and slow down as needed, and you can emphasize the rhyming words with your voice.

Once your child is familiar with the rhyme, use a natural pause to see if they will say the next word.

For example:

Incy wincy spider climbed up the water spout

Down came the rain and washed the spider... (Pause and look expectant- give 5 seconds then fill in the word for your child if they don't say it).

Make rhyming into a game: I'm thinking of a word that rhymes with something in the kitchen. My word is 'hair'. What am I thinking of?

When your child is a little older, you can start to explain rhyme- "these words sound the same- they have the same ending."

Syllables

Make syllables into a game: Clap out the syllables in the names in your family, or clap out the syllables in the things that you see while on a walk, at dinner time, or any time that works for you.

For example:

Look a butterfly! Let's clap it- bu/tter/fly

A caterpillar- ready to clap it- ca/ter/pill/ar

Try to make this game fun and interesting, and not a 'lesson.'

Sound Hunt

Go on a 'Sound Hunt' in the house or garden- how many things beginning with 'mm' can you find.

Remember that the sound of a letter and the name of the letter are very different things.

You can raise your child's awareness of this by finding opportunities to highlight it.

For example:

"oh, a spider- that starts with a sssss- sssspider. That sound is called S."

Or "that starts with a letter M- that letter makes the sound- mmmm."

However, be aware that finding something beginning with a sound is more difficult that listening to a word and determining if it begins with the sound.

Create a Collage

Create a collage of pictures with just one sound. Cut things out from magazines and papers that have the sound you want.

Have fun using the target sound during a craft. If your target sound is "S Blends", you could build a crafty snowman. Target sounds could
include: snow, snowball, scarf, scary, smile, sparkles, stick, st ones, stars, slippery, and stomach.

Speech Bag

Create a speech bag by collecting small objects that contain the target sound.

Use the bag to play guessing games with your child (you describe what is inside the bag and they guess what object it is- one clue will be: 'it starts with the sound...')

ABOUT THE AUTHOR

Freya works as a Speech and Language Pathologist. She loves coaching parents and teachers in using language intervention strategies within daily routines. She loves learning and taking on new challenges. She is the face behind HappierWithTea.com where she blogs about parenting, work and wellness. Her favorite thing is to escape the world with a good book and a cup of tea in hand.

You can find her on her blog where she writes about parenting, wellness.

HappierWithTea.com

BOOST YOUR CHILD'S LANGUAGE: AN ESSENTIAL GUIDE FOR PARENTS

Freya Magennis

What you need to know to get your child talking!

This guide will give you lots of easy ways to get your child talking. Whether you have a toddler who isn't saying much yet, or an older child, these ideas can be easily adjusted for any level!

This is the parent's guide to speech and language therapy- an essential parenting tool to support your child's speech and language development.

This book recognizes the role that you as a parent play in your child's language development and is filled with simple and practical ideas of the most important things you can do as a parent, as well as giving you a better understanding of how language develops and what to expect at different ages.

The strategies outlined in this book are designed to be used throughout your everyday activities and experiences with your child.

Get your copy from Amazon!

Made in the USA
Coppell, TX
19 March 2022

75227783R00032